STRESS RELIEVING ADULT COLORING BOOK

A Coloring Book For Adults Featuring Designs, Patterns, and Motivational Quotes For Relaxation, Inspiration & Happiness

LIFESTYLEDEZIGN

LIFESTYLEDEZIGN

Lifestyle Dezign Coloring is located in Phoenix, AZ.

© 2015 Lifestyle Dezign
All rights reserved.

Proudly printed in the United States of America

It's as Easy As 1, 2, 3…

1 De-stress: Find somewhere quiet, calming, and distraction free.

2 Detox from Digitals: Turn off all electronics and place them out of sight or in another room.

3 Design: Pull out your colored pencils or crayons, relax, be inspired, and let your imagination run wild.

Happy Coloring!

"No matter what happens to you in your life, you alone have the capacity to choose your response to it. When you form the habit of searching for the positive in every circumstance, your life will move into its highest dimensions. This is one of the greatest of all the natural laws."

- Robin Sharma

"The first recipe for happiness is: avoid lengthy meditation on the past."

- Andre Maurois

"And remember, no matter where you go, there you are."

- Confucious

"If you are too busy to laugh, you are too busy."

- Proverb

"Learn to let go. That is the key to happiness."

- Buddha

"Be like a lotus. Let the beauty of your heart speak. Be greatful to the mud, water, air, and the light."

- Amit Ray

"The smallest of actions is always better than the noblest of intentions."

- Robin Sharma

"On a deeper level you are already complete. When you realize that, there is a playful, joyous energy behind what you do."

- Eckhart Tolle

"Optimism is a happiness magnet. If you stay positive, good things and good people will be drawn to you."

- Mary Lou Retton

"I believe compassion to be one of the few things we can practice that will bring immediate and long term happiness to our lives."

- Dalai Lama

"Investing in yourself is the best investment you will ever make. It will not only improve your life, it will improve the lives of all those around you."

- Robin Sharma

"He who knows others is wise.
He who knows himself is enlightened."

- Lao Tzu

"One of the greatest lessons that adults can learn from children is the enviable ability to find happiness with simplicity."

- Summer Jeirles

"At the core of your heart, you are perfect and pure. No one and nothing can alter that."

- Amit Ray

"Give out what you most want to come back."

- Robin Sharma

"The grass is always greener where you water it."

- Unknown

"Follow your bliss and don't be afraid, and doors will open where you didn't know they were going to be."

- Joseph Campbell

"The greatest gift is a portion of thyself."

- Ralph Waldo Emerson

"Stop, breathe, look around and embrace the miracle of life."

- Jeffrey White

"To be fully aware means to be fully aware now, at this moment.
There is no past.
There is no future.
There is only now."

- Gourasana

"Feelings come and go like clouds in the sky. Conscious breathing is my anchor."

- Thich Nhat Hanh

"The most fundamental aggression to ourselves, the most fundamental harm we can do to ourselves, is to remain ignorant by not having the courage and the respect to look at ourselves honestly and gently."

- Chodron

"If you want to conquer the anxiety of life, live in the moment, live in the breath."

- Amit Ray

"In the end, just three things matter:
How well we have lived
How well we have loved
How well we have learned to let go."

- Jack Kornfield

"Do every act of your life as though it were the very last act of your life."

- Marcus Aurelius

"Few of us ever live in the present. We are forever anticipating what is to come or remembering what has gone."

- Louis L'Amour

**"Perfection of character is this:
To live each day as if it were your last, without frenzy, without apathy, without pretence."**

- Marcus Aurelius

"In this moment, there is plenty of time. In this moment, you are precisely as you should be. In this moment, there is infinite possibility."

- Victoria Moran

"There are a thousand reasons to live this life, everyone of them sufficient."

- Marilynne Robinson

"Mind is a flexible mirror, adjust it, to see a better world."

- Amit Ray

"Never regret your past. Rather, embrace it as the teacher that it is."

- Robin Sharma

"Breath is the finest gift of nature. Be grateful for this wonderful gift."

- Amit Ray

**"Respond, don't react.
Listen, don't talk.
Think, don't assume."**

- Raji Lukkoor

"Meditation is the ultimate mobile device; you can use it anywhere, anytime, unobtrusively."

- Sharon Salzberg

"Worry drains the mind of its power and, sooner or later, it injures the soul."

- Robin Sharma

"Big people don't make people feel small."

- Robin Sharma

"Meditate, visualize and create your own reality and the universe will simply reflect back to you."

- Amit Ray

"Meditation is a microcosm, a model, a mirror. The skills we practice when we sit are transferable to the rest of our lives."

- Sharon Salzberg

"When you reach a calm and quiet meditative state, that is when you can hear the sound of silence."

- Stephen Richards

"Inner peace can be seen as the ultimate benefit of practicing patience."

- Buddha

Thank you for joining the movement to bring relaxation, inspiration, and happiness into the lives of adults everywhere. Join our community of amazing colorists for tips, inspiration, to learn about our commitment to giving back, and to showcase your beautiful art!

facebook.com/lifestyledezigncoloring

@LDColoring

@lifestyledezigncoloring

pinterest.com/lifestyledezign

Now it's your turn to let your imagination go wild. Have fun drawing your own creative art and adding your illustrations to this book!

STRESS RELIEVING ADULT COLORING BOOK

STRESS RELIEVING ADULT COLORING BOOK

STRESS RELIEVING ADULT COLORING BOOK

STRESS RELIEVING ADULT COLORING BOOK

STRESS RELIEVING ADULT COLORING BOOK

www.ingramcontent.com/pod-product-compliance
Lightning Source LLC
Chambersburg PA
CBHW081220020426

42331CB00012B/3053